Family Walks
in Snowdonia

Laurence Main

HIGH INTEREST · LOW MILEAGE

Scarthin Books of Cromford
Derbyshire
1998

A

Family Walks Series

General Editor: Norman Taylor

WALKING THE ROUTES IN THIS BOOK
All the routes in this book have been walked, in most cases, several times prior to publication and we have taken great care to ensure that they are on rights of way. However, changes occur all the time in the landscape; should you meet any obstructions, please let us know. Serious obstructions can be brought to the attention of the local branch of the Ramblers Association and the Rights of Way section of the County Council.

THE COUNTRYSIDE CODE

Guard against all risk of fire
Fasten all gates
Keep dogs under proper control
Keep to the paths across farmland
Avoid damaging fences, hedges and walls
Leave no litter
Safeguard water supplies
Protect wildlife, wild plants and trees
Go carefully on country roads
Respect the life of the countryside

Published by Scarthin Books, Cromford, Derbyshire.

Phototypesetting, printing by Higham Press Ltd., Shirland, Derbyshire

Cover photograph by the Author.
Route 13, overlooking Dinas Mawddwy.

© Laurence Main 1990, reprinted 1993, 1994, 1996, 1998.

ISBN 0 907758 32 0

Looking towards Snowdon   (Route 2)

1

Preface

"Perhaps in the whole world there is no region more picturesquely beautiful than Snowdonia, a region of mountains, lakes, cataracts and groves in which nature shows herself in her most grand and beautiful form." That was written in 1854 by George Borrow, who walked across many lands. Borrow was also able to surprise the natives by speaking in their own tongue. Welsh is still spoken by three-quarters of the people who live within the boundary of the National Park, giving a holiday here an exotic flavour. Even the public footpath signposts keep pointing to somewhere called "Llwybr Cyhoeddus" (actually, this is Welsh for "public footpath" but visitors have stopped me to ask where this elusive place was on their map). But is Snowdonia a place for families to walk? After all, not everybody feels up to climbing over 3,000 feet with a baby in a papoose or a complaining youngster. Don't worry, the babies adore the rarefied atmosphere, while their older brothers and sisters enjoy the freedom of the hills. There's nothing wrong with a cautious, gentle start, however. These selected routes will give you that and whet your appetite for more.

Acknowledgements

I would like to thank Janet Davies for the help given in reaching some of these walks. Others (unknown) were kind enough to give me lifts (I live away from the main bus routes). Tom Jones, a local farmer, introduced me to the Llynnau Gregennen and to Basil and Dorothy Sayle, the present inhabitants of Park Cottage (Route 12). The Meirionnydd District Library at Dolgellau gave its usual excellent service. Two of my children, David and Chantal, tested the walks. I would like to dedicate this book to their sister, Michelle Rhiannon, who was born as it was nearing completion.

About the author

Born and educated in Oxford, Laurence Main worked as a teacher in Swindon for six years before becoming the Assistant Secretary and Education Officer of the Vegan Society in 1980. A year later, he moved to Dinas Mawddwy, in Meirionnydd, and was responsible for the bio-fuel display funded by the Vegan Society at the Centre for Alternative Technology, Machynlleth. He is now a full-time walk leader and writer of footpath guides, including "The Dyfi Valley Way" (Bartholomew Kittiwake) and "Walk Snowdonia and North Wales" (Bartholomew). He is the Ramblers' Association's Footpaths Secretary for Meirionnydd.

Contents

Location Map of the Walks

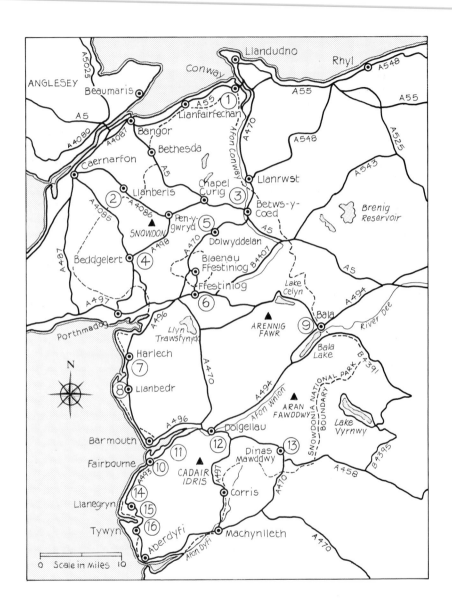

Introduction

This is a book of walks that are especially suitable for families. Hardened backpackers and experienced ramblers are catered for in other books, but here are the relatively short and undemanding walks that will be appreciated by a parent carrying a papoose or a child with young legs. Each has its own special feature that will attract and stimulate young minds. This may be a woodland walk through a National Nature Reserve, a visit to a spectacular waterfall or a riverside or lakeside stroll. The walks also encounter steam railways, a native Welsh castle, Edward I's castles, ancient standing stones and a stone circle. A variety of museums and other tourist attractions are visited, including a Lightship and an old R.A.F. camp complete with a Spitfire. This is also mysterious Wales, with famous legends, Celtic saints, a lake monster, a sorcerer who raised the devil, an authentic murder scene, fairies and a girl whose trek for a copy of the Bible was to inspire an international organisation. Above all, this is a land of majestic scenery, from the highest mountains to the seashore.

Walking and close contact with the real, living world is an essential part of growing up, especially in the age of television. Walking is a natural activity which requires little in the way of money and gives enjoyment without any competitive element. It is ideal for families, who do not need to join a club in order to do it. The walking season never ends, indeed each month brings its own character and invites you to repeat a walk at different times of the year. The winter is often the best time for a short, brisk walk, as long as commonsense prevails regarding the weather, precautions and clothing.

Snowdonia is the second largest national park in Great Britain. Its 845 square miles make only a slightly smaller area than the 866 square miles of the English Lake District. Snowdon is the highest mountain south of the Scottish Highlands, at 3,560 ft. Come between Easter and September and you will hardly need a guide up Snowdon — just join the queue. Half a million souls every year gain spiritual sustenance by climbing it. You won't have the same problem on the other high peaks, which all require the greatest respect should you venture up them. This book reserves the mountains for magnificent background scenery. The highest you'll go is 1,100 ft — high enough to acquire a taste for such adventure. The views are breathtaking, especially over the sea, while the moorland is desolate. Some slopes are steep, including those on an apparently easy walk at Harlech.

The National Park is more than the mountains. Some of the finest coastal beaches in Great Britain lie within its borders, as does the largest lake in Wales. The Bryncrug walk follows an embankment above the light and delicate reeds and grasses of the Afon Dysynni, famous for its herons. Similarly, the line of the dismantled railway east of Morfa Mawddach provides a corridor through the wildlife habitats beside the Mawddach Estuary. The original climax vegetation for nearly all of Snowdonia, up to the 2000 ft contour, was Sessile Oak forest, This is nearly all gone, the victim of overgrazing by sheep. Hence the value of the small, steep and secluded valleys, such as at Ceunant Cynfal, which escaped being spoiled. Plantations of alien conifers have also changed the landscape. If they represent the triumph (?) of Man over Nature, the real success has been achieved by the rampant rhododendron. Try the Dinas Mawddwy walk in June for a memorable display of pink across the valley from your track.

Most of these walks are in the southern half of Snowdonia, in Meirionnydd. This is only fair as so many other books of walks in the national park seem to forget that Meirionnydd exists. In fact, this is the better part of Snowdonia. The scenery is as interesting and exciting, but the crowds of tourists are thinner and the traffic jams shorter. The discerning walker will head for Meirionnydd rather than the better known area immediately around Snowdon. This won't mean much of a sacrifice in terms of grandeur. Cadair Idris is 2,928 ft, while Aran Fawddwy (surprisingly, to most people) is even higher at 2,971 ft. All types of accommodation and other facilities are widely available, but Dolgellau is a good central location. It is a hub of the commendable Bws Gwynedd network, on the route of the Traws Cambria bus from Cardiff and of buses from Wrexham. There is much to be said for British Rail's Cambrian Coast Line, however, with Harlech offering a campsite, an indoor heated swimming pool and a theatre.

One way would be to plan a tour, threading the walks together. You could start with walk 1, then go round walks 2, 4, 7, 8, 12, 11, 10, 14, 15, 16, 13, 9, 6, 5 and 3. If you are absolute beginners, it would be wise to try walks 3, 4, 8, 9, 10 and 15 first. You could then keep walks 1, 2, 6, 11 and 14 until you are experienced. Don't be afraid to cut a walk short or to retrace your steps, especially if the weather worsens or the sun starts to sink below the horizon. Allow for a pace of one mile an hour. Equip your child with stout shoes and an anorak. Avoid jeans (which are very uncomfortable if soaked) and opt for several thin layers of clothing rather than one heavy jersey. A rucksack will be needed to carry spare clothes as well as your picnic, camera and maps.

Make a practice of carrying the relevant Ordnance Survey Outdoor Leisure map (at a scale of $2\frac{1}{2}$ ins to 1 mile). Snowdonia is covered by sheets 16, 17, 18 and 23. Older children could be taught to use a compass, while a torch is another useful item to carry. Bring some food and drink even if refreshments are available locally. Many places only open during the tourist season.

Some of the most delightful moments are when you meet a friendly farmer. This is when your knowledge of, or just willingness to learn, Welsh will stand you in good stead. Please don't bring dogs on to sheep pasture.

The Welsh Language

Welsh is a living language spoken by half a million people just a few miles away from English cities such as Liverpool, Birmingham and Bristol. There are also many Welsh-speakers living in England. Yet the Welsh language is virtually ignored on the eastern side of Offa's Dyke and schools arrange costly trips across the Channel in order to convince their pupils that other people like to speak their own language in preference to English. In the past, English conquerors despised the Welsh language, the oldest living language in Europe, and Welsh history, with its great relevance to the ancient past of our shared island. Some knowledge of, and respect for, the language will greatly increase your enjoyment of walking in Snowdonia, the final bastion of independent Wales.

About 24,000 people live in Snowdonia and some 18,000 of them speak Welsh. There are still many adults to whom English is a strange, foreign tongue. Some valleys are so remote that the children didn't bother to attend school (where English was imposed), especially during the Second World War when there weren't the school taxis. Remoteness has never stopped learning, of course, and education has always taken pride of place in Wales. So too, especially in Snowdonia, has a sense of national identity. Institutions such as the chapel and the eisteddfod have all helped to foster the language. Now the schools are the main hope for the future of Welsh. More and more English migrants are putting at risk the predominance of the old tongue. Their children can be taught to become fluent Welsh-speakers, however. Even you could learn a few words and phrases. Try these:

Good morning — Bore da (bor-eh-da)
Good afternoon — Prynhawn da (Pre-noun-da)
Good evening — Noswaith da (Noss-wa-eeth-da)
Please — Os gwelwch yn dda (Oss-gwe-loo-kin-tha)
Thank you very much — Diolch yn fawr (Dee-olc-hen-vawr)

Symbols used on the route maps

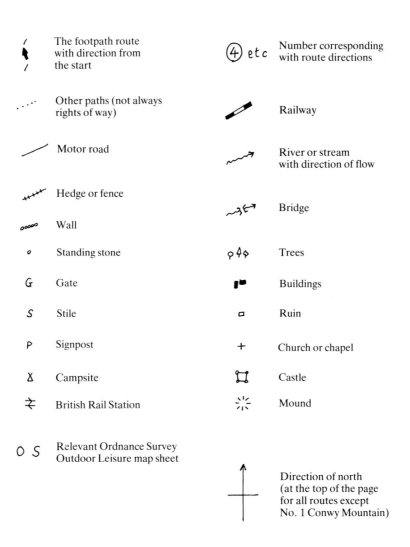

The footpath route with direction from the start	Number corresponding with route directions ④ etc
Other paths (not always rights of way)	Railway
Motor road	River or stream with direction of flow
Hedge or fence	Bridge
Wall	
o Standing stone	Trees
G Gate	Buildings
S Stile	Ruin
P Signpost	Church or chapel
Ӽ Campsite	Castle
British Rail Station	Mound
O S Relevant Ordnance Survey Outdoor Leisure map sheet	Direction of north (at the top of the page for all routes except No. 1 Conwy Mountain)

Each map has a scale in miles and a gradient profile showing the height in feet above sea level and the distance in miles from the start of the walk.

Conwy Mountain

Outline
Conwy Castle - Conwy Visitor Centre - Conwy Mountain - Plas Mawr - Conwy Harbour - Conwy Castle.

Summary
A delightful medieval town is the base for a walk along good tracks to a hill (Conwy Mountain is only 808 feet high) with magnificent views of Snowdonia, the Great Orme and of Conwy, whose castle guides you back to a series of tourist attractions which will keep you here all day.

Attractions
Visitors from England will probably have reached Conwy by one of the bridges across the picturesque Conwy Estuary, although the A55 will soon take a tunnel under the river. The middle bridge is a suspension bridge built by Thomas Telford in 1826, while the railway uses Robert Stephenson's tubular girder bridge, opened in 1846. These lead to Conwy Castle, which was erected by Edward I between 1283 and 1287 at a cost of £14,000 (at least £5 million by today's prices). This was Edward's most expensive castle and he needed its walls to defend him from the Welsh when they rose up under Madog in 1295. The town walls are remarkably well-preserved and can add an extra mile to this walk. Enclosed within them are equally old buildings.

A visit to the castle is highly recommended and it includes an impressive exhibition at the entrance. Conwy has another Visitor Centre just before the station is passed on your left. Perhaps you should leave this until after the walk as it has film shows as well as exhibitions to portray Conwy's history. On your return to Lancaster Square from Conwy Mountain, this route passes Plas Mawr. Acknowledged as the finest Elizabethan town house in Wales and now an art gallery and headquarters of the Royal Cambrian Academy of Art, you will have to pay your admission fee to learn the legend of the Lantern Room.

Aberconwy House is next and even older, dating from the 14th century. Now in the care of the National Trust, it contains an exhibition about Conwy from Roman times, when there was a legionary outpost on Conwy Mountain and the Afon Conwy was famous for its pearl fisheries. Conwy Harbour is now the venue for boat trips, while the Conwy Harbour Lightship is moored here for visitors to board. The "Smallest House in Great Britain" is also on the quay, near the Aquarium. No wonder Conwy is such a popular tourist attraction!

9

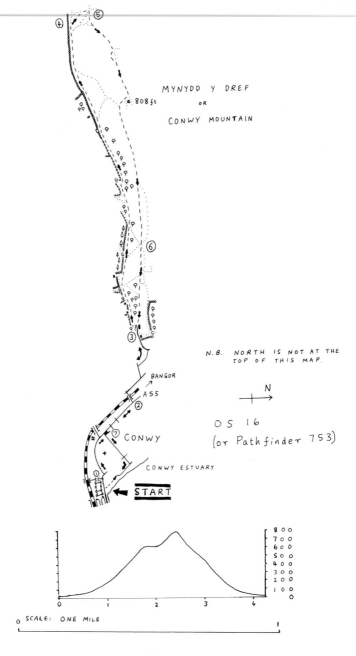

MYNYDD Y DREF
OR
CONWY MOUNTAIN

808ft

④ ⑤

⑥

③

N.B. NORTH IS NOT AT THE
TOP OF THIS MAP.

BANGOR
A55
②

N

⑦ CONWY

OS 16
(or Pathfinder 753)

CONWY ESTUARY

① **START**

SCALE: ONE MILE

Route 1

Conwy Mountain $4\frac{1}{4}$ miles

Start

Conwy is easy to reach by train, bus or car. It has a station on British Rail's line from Chester to Holyhead and is served by several buses. Motorists can reach here on the A55 and choose from one of the signposted car parks. The castle is easy to find, being prominent, near the station and the bridges across the Afon Conwy. Start from the entrance to the castle, which is signposted as a Tourist Information Centre. It is across a side street from the castle, which visitors reach by taking a footbridge. (G.R. SH783775)

Route

1. *Go left up Rose Hill Street, passing the Conwy Visitor Centre and the station on your left. Continue past Lancaster Square and through a gate in the town walls along the Bangor Road.*

2. *Turn left at Cadnant Park to cross the railway cutting and bear right until Mountain Road. Turn right up Mountain Road, bearing left at a road junction.*

3. *Mountain Road peters out at some cottages. Fork left just before them to follow the signposted path which passes three houses on your left, then runs beside a wall. Do not bear left with the fence after the wall, but go ahead along the main track past trees and with a fence which soon becomes a wall on your left. Continue to where several paths cross a pass on the right.*

4. *Bear right along the main path to reach a crossroads of paths, where there is a view across the bay to the Great Orme ahead of you.*

5. *Turn right here to walk with the sea on your left and follow the main path along the mountain back to Conwy, whose castle and bridges soon make a picturesque view ahead.*

6. *At a crossroads of paths above Conwy take care to descend gradually with the main path ahead, passing above the trees on your right to reach the cottages which mark the start of Mountain Road. Retrace your steps to Lancaster Square in the centre of Conwy.*

7. *Turn left up the High Street, soon passing Plas Mawr on your left. Pass Aberconwy House on your right at the corner with Castle Street and go ahead through a gate in the town walls to Conwy Harbour, with the landing stage ahead of you, the Smallest House on your left, and the Aquarium on your right. Turn right to pass the Conwy Harbour Lightship and return to the castle.*

Public Transport

There is a good train service to Conwy from Chester or Holyhead, including through trains from Llandudno. Sunday services are less frequent, but it's not far across Conwy Bridge to Llandudno Junction. Conwy is well-served by buses, including on Sundays.

The X1 Limited Stop bus along the North Wales coast stops here, as does the slower No. 5 bus between Llandudno and Caernarfon. Traffic follows a one way route around the town, so catch eastbound buses in Castle Street and westbound buses at Lancaster Square.

Refreshments
There is plenty of choice in Conwy to suit all tastes and pockets.

Conwy Harbour

Llanberis

Outline
Snowdon Mountain Railway Terminus - Coed Victoria - Capel Hebron - Snowdon Mountain Railway Terminus.

Summary
This route follows clear tracks above the village to provide views of Snowdon as well as Llyn Padarn and Llanberis.

Attractions
The Snowdon Mountain Railway was built to take families to the summit of the highest mountain in Wales and England. You'll want to walk up to the summit, of course (and many young children can be seen doing so), but the train ride is highly recommended as well. The routes to the summit are well documented elsewhere, so this is a less ambitious walk designed to whet young appetites by giving excellent views on a fine day and introducing them to the atmosphere of this famous peak.

The Snowdon Mountain Railway is the only rack railway in Britain. It runs for 4½ miles from Llanberis to Snowdon's summit, climbing 3,140 feet in the process (Snowdon is 3560 feet high). The mountain demands great respect and the construction of the railway up it was accompanied by an unfortunate incident, akin to a blood sacrifice. On the railway's opening day, in 1896, there was a fatal accident. The locomotive was then pulling the carriages, so that when a carriage broke away it was free to run downhill. The coach was to be halted by its automatic brakes, but not before one of the pioneers had jumped out in panic — to his death.

The railway's narrow gauge of 2ft 7½ ins. seems to keep it in its place, a curious midget which gives a great deal of enjoyment. The "slum" at the summit has long been deplored, however. At least you'll find refreshments available during the season. Perhaps it is more appealing than the German beer-garden that Frank Smythe had a nightmarish vision of in 1941, when Hitler was far from beaten. Mercifully, few have attempted to emulate Sir William Letts' feat of driving to the summit in a light automobile in 1903. One worthy ascent was made by the father of Dr. William Temple, recorded when his son was Archbishop of York in 1933. He'd already made five ascents in five days, when he made a sixth to pay 6d for a bottle of ginger-beer which he'd remembered not paying for. There was no train when George Borrow climbed Snowdon, as recorded in his book "Wild Wales" (1862). He reminded his step-daughter of the lines in the 'Day of Judgement', by the illustrious Goronwy Owen:

"The brow of Snowdon shall be levelled with the ground,
  and the eddying waters shall murmur round it."

13

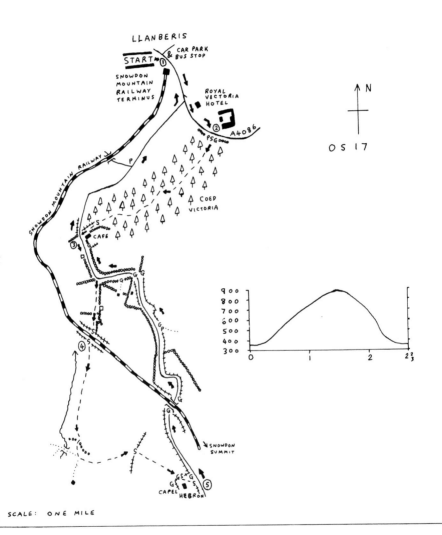

LLANBERIS

START

CAR PARK
& BUS STOP

SNOWDON
MOUNTAIN
RAILWAY
TERMINUS

ROYAL
VICTORIA
HOTEL

A4086

PSG

SNOWDON MOUNTAIN RAILWAY

P

COED
VICTORIA

S
CAFE

G

GP

S

SNOWDON
SUMMIT

S

GS G S

G S
CAPEL HEBRON

N

OS 17

900
800
700
600
500
400
300

0   1   2   2⅔

SCALE: ONE MILE

14

Route 2

Llanberis   2⅔ miles

Start

Llanberis is on the A4086 eight miles east of Caernarfon. Look for the Snowdon Mountain Railway's terminus on your right as you go towards Capel Curig. There is a car park on your left, while buses also stop here. (G.R. SH583598)

Route

1. With your back to the station, go right along the pavement of the A4086 towards Capel Curig. Pass a road turning on your right and pass the Royal Victoria Hotel on your left.

2. Turn right to cross a stile and follow a forest track. This winds uphill to reach a stile between a wall and a fence. Go ahead across it to reach a lane.

3. Go left along the lane, past a seasonal cafe on your left, to a bend. When the road bends left, turn right to follow a path running beside a wall on your left. Go ahead to a stile which gives access to the mountain railway. Cross this carefully and continue over another stile.

4. Keep straight on along a moorland path until you are level with a bridge across a stream on your right. Turn left here to face Snowdon and walk towards it. Cross a stile in a new fence and proceed to a stile beside a gate at Capel Hebron. This chapel is now disused and too dangerous to enter. Continue to the stile which gives access to the lane.

5. Turn left down the lane. Follow it under a railway bridge and back to the cafe passed on the way up. Instead of turning into the forest on your right, continue descending along the lane. When it joins the A4086, turn left back to the Snowdon Mountain Railway terminus.

Refreshments

Llanberis has a choice of places offering refreshments. The cafe on the route is open on a seasonal basis, as is the cafe at the Snowdon Mountain Railway terminus.

Public Transport

Llanberis is well served by buses from Caernarfon (Nos. 88 and 98, including Sundays). The Snowdon Mountain Railway is seasonal, usually from March to October (tel. 01286 870223 for details).

By the Afon Conwy

Betws-y-Coed

Outline
Railway Station - Conwy Valley Railway Museum -Afon Conwy - Afon Llugwy - Royal Oak Stables & Visitor Centre - Railway Station.

Summary
This short walk covers very easy ground, while children of all ages will find something to absorb their interest, so allow plenty of time to complete it. The bulk of the route follows the banks of the Afon Conwy and Afon Llugwy, around the edge of a golf course. The Railway Museum is highly recommended, while the Visitor Centre will greatly enhance your enjoyment of Snowdonia.

Attractions
Betws-y-Coed has an Alpine setting, surrounded by the Gwydyr Forest. Artists find it particularly inspiring, with the Birmingham watercolourist David Cox's name being particularly linked with the area. The village is also a natural communications centre, situated at the junction of the Conwy, Llugwy and Lledr valleys. The Conwy Valley Line is still part of the Railway network, having carried hordes of Victorian tourists to this spot. Many of them stayed at the Royal Oak Hotel, whose old stables now house the Visitor Centre. An excellent exhibition is augmented by an audio-visual presentation.

This is also a sacred spot. Betws-y-Coed means "Chapel in the Wood" and a clue to the reason for such a building being located here lies in the name of the "old church" which this route passes. This 14th century church is dedicated to St. Michael and All Angels. Dowsers have discovered that churches dedicated to St. Michael occur on or near leys, alignments of ancient sites akin to the old celtic "fairy paths". Further research may indicate the existence of "Michael" and "Mary" lines spiralling around the straight leys. Where their "masculine" and "feminine" loops meet may be significant places of spiritual power or windows into other dimensions. It so happens that the "old church" of St. Michael, now used just for funerals, has been replaced as the parish church by St. Mary's, on the other side of the railway and the A5.

The Conwy Valley Railway Museum is well worth the admission fee. It houses delightful dioramas depicting the old London and North Western Railway, models and railwayana. Take a ride on the 7¼ gauge railway which passes close to its British Rail counterpart. Refreshments are available in a buffet car. If you have come here by Railway, there is a direct footbridge access between the station and the museum. Motorists can find a car park between the Visitor Centre and the Motor Museum.

Route 3

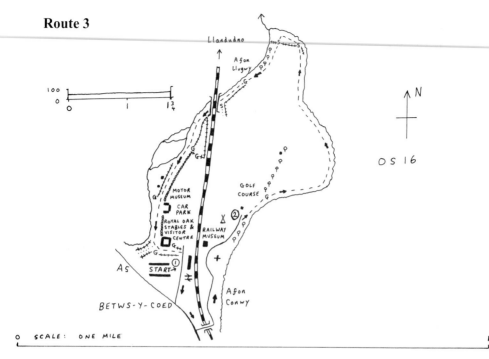

Near Betws-Y-Coed

18

Route 3

Betws-y-Coed 1¾ miles

Start

Betws-y-Coed is easy to reach, having a station on the Conwy Valley Line and being at the junction of the A5 and the A470. This walk starts from the entrance to the station, near which is a car park. (G.R. SH795566)

Route

1. *With your back to the station, go left to reach the A5. Turn left along this main road until the first turning on your left, signposted to a golf course. Take this lane, crossing a bridge over the railway. Pass St. Michael's church on your right and the Railway Museum on your left. Go ahead towards the golf course.*

2. *Just before the end of the lane, take the footpath on your right which follows the bank of the Afon Conwy. With the river on your right, go ahead through a kissing gate and around the edge of the golf course. Just before the Afon Conwy's confluence with its tributary, the Afon Llugwy, follow the path over two stiles. Walk upstream beside the Afon Llugwy on your right. Continue under a railway bridge and on past the Motor Museum on your left to the Visitor Centre. Bear left back to the start.*

Refreshments

Betws-y-Coed has several places offering refreshments, but why not patronise the Buffet Coach Cafe at the Conwy Valley Railway Museum?

Public Transport

Trains from Llandudno or Blaenau Ffestiniog will take you to the start of this walk. Betws-y-Coed is also on several bus routes.

Beddgelert

20

Beddgelert

Outline
Royal Goat Hotel - Gelert's Grave - Dismantled Railway Bridge - Royal Goat Hotel.

Summary
This short, gentle walk is a great favourite with families. The supposed grave of Gelert is the prime attraction, but the peaceful path beside the Afon Glaslyn hardly needs such an incentive for people to tread along it. The whole is set in magnificent scenery, while a touch of nostalgia is brought by the fact that the southern footbridge across the river is set within the bridge of the dismantled Welsh Highland Railway. Navigation is so simple that you can just relax and enjoy this one!

Attractions
Of all the Welsh legends, the story of how Gelert the greyhound was killed by his own master must be the one most familiar to English children. How then, could a family visit Snowdonia and not visit the grave of such an unfortunate beast? That must have been the reasoning of David Prichard, the landlord of the Royal Goat Hotel, when he set up a cairn to Gelert's supposed grave in 1801. He was making the connection between the greyhound's name and that of his village. Beddgelert does mean Gelert's grave, but this is most probably a reference to the Celtic saint Celert. A Celtic monastery flourished here when the Afon Glaslyn was an important channel for sea-going boats. St. Mary's church is a remnant of a medieval Augustinian priory. It is the large slate slab shaded by a sycamore tree which marks Gelert's grave, however. The story is briefly retold on this slab, while fuller versions are available in any number of books. Llywelyn ab Iorwerth, Prince of Wales in the 13th century, spent the summer hunting here. His favourite hound was the faithful Gelert. One day Llywelyn went out hunting, leaving his baby son in the charge of its nurse. The nurse risked leaving the baby on its own in the hunting-lodge while she went for a walk in the woods with her boyfriend. Llywelyn, meanwhile, noticed that his faithful hound Gelert had disappeared from the hunting-pack. Returning home, he found Gelert covered in blood, his son's cradle overturned and the baby missing. Assuming that Gelert had killed his son, Llywelyn struck the hound a mortal blow with his sword. As the dog gave its last yelp, however, the baby cried and Llywelyn realised the truth. Gelert had rushed back, sensing the need to protect his master's son and heir. A wolf had attacked the child and its dead body lay under the bedclothes. The remorseful Llywelyn buried Gelert on this spot, marking the grave with stones. A sad tale, but with a moral to it!

Route 4

Footbridge over Afon Glaslyn

22

Route 4
Beddgelert
1¾ miles

Start

Beddgelert is at the junction of the A498 and the A4085. Start from the Royal Goat Hotel, which is on your left as you approach the village from the south. A car park and bus stop are nearby. (G.R. SH588481)

Route

1. *With your back to the Royal Goat Hotel, go left along the main A498 road into the village. When this bears left across a bridge over the Afon Colwyn, leave it by continuing straight ahead with the river on your left. This lane leads to a footbridge ahead across the Afon Glaslyn. Instead of proceeding across this bridge, turn right just before it and go through a gate to walk downstream with the river on your left. Reach a wall ahead on your right and turn right to walk with the wall on your left as far as a gap in it. Bear left through this to see Gelert's grave.*

2. *Retrace your steps to the riverside path and bear right along it, maintaining your previous direction. Reach a footbridge on your left, set within an old Welsh Highland Railway bridge, and turn left over it.*

3. *Turn left to walk upstream with the river on your left. Reach the village and turn left across the footbridge over the Afon Glaslyn. Retrace your steps to the start.*

Refreshments

Beddgelert has a choice of places offering refreshments.

Public Transport

Beddgelert can be reached by bus from Porthmadog (No. 97), Caernarfon (No. 11), Pwllheli (No. 55 — an infrequent service through to and from Shrewsbury) and Llandudno (No. 19 — an infrequent service).

Dolwyddelan Castle

Dolwyddelan Castle

Outline
Car Park - Dolwyddelan Castle - Roman Bridge Station - Dolwyddelan Castle - Car Park.

Summary
Dolwyddelan Castle has its own car park beside the A470 about one mile south-west of the village of Dolwyddelan. The best way to come here is by train, on the scenic Conwy Valley Line (between Llandudno and Blaenau Ffestiniog). The nearest station is at Roman Bridge, so this walk continues to it. Motorists needn't go all the way, of course, but this arrangement allows train passengers to join the walk. Whatever you do, avoid walking along the busy A470. This is a fairly gentle walk along a good track which provides magnificent views. You are on your honour to pay your admission fee for visiting Dolwyddelan Castle at Bryn Tirion, from where the key can be collected.

Attractions
When King Edward I conquered Wales he suppressed resistance in Snowdonia by building the great castles, such as Caernarfon and Conwy, for which Wales is now famous. Their enormous construction costs were a tribute to the fiercely independent spirit of Gwynedd and the rugged nature of the terrain. By contrast, the castles erected by the native Welsh princes to defend their territory were mean and are relatively unknown. Dolwyddelan is a fine example, prominently guarding the principal routeway through Snowdonia along the Lledr valley from Nant Conwy to Meirionnydd. It was originally built by Iorwerth of the Broken Nose in about 1170 and was the birthplace of Llywelyn the Great, who was to control nearly all Wales by 1215. Llywelyn replaced the earlier motte with a rectangular tower which was impressive by Welsh standards. This was captured by Edward I in 1283. By 1488 it had passed into the hands of Maredudd ab Ieuan, descendant of the Princes of Powys and ancestor of the Wynns of Gwydir Castle. The castle subsequently fell into disrepair, but its upper parts were restored in the 19th century. The building houses an exhibition, while there is a splendid view of Moel Siabod (2,861 ft) from the battlements.

Route 5

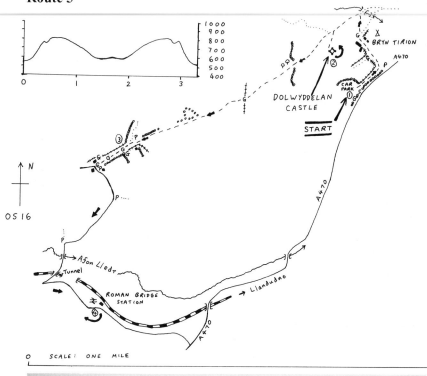

Route 5

Dolwyddelan Castle

$3\frac{1}{3}$ miles

Start

Motorists should start from the car park below Dolwyddelan Castle on your right if you drive south-westwards from Dolwyddelan village (towards Blaenau Ffestiniog) along the A470. (G.R. SH723522) If you come by train, join the walk at Roman Bridge Station. (G.R. SH713514)

Route

1. Face the castle, with your back to the A470 and go right along the marked path to Dolwyddelan Castle. This goes between a fence on your left and a wall on your right. It then bears left to Bryn Tirion, where you should pay for admission to the castle and collect the key. Take a gate on your right and climb the path on your left to join another track just before a bridge, where a sign directs you to the castle on your left.

2. Having visited the castle, return to the track and turn sharply left to follow a clear track which goes through a gap in the wall ahead. Continue along it through a gate in a fence and past a broken wall on your right to a signpost.

3. Go ahead through gates and between a wall and a fence to reach a lane at another signpost. Go left downhill, following the lane across the Afon Lledr, the Conwy Valley railway and round a sharp bend on the left to British Rail's Roman Bridge Station.

4. If you are a motorist, simply retrace your steps (avoid the A470). If you travel by train, start the walk here by turning right from the station, following the lane round a sharp right bend and crossing the railway near the entrance to a tunnel on your right. Continue along the lane over a bridge across the Afon Lledr and uphill, ignoring a signposted path on your left, then another signposted path on your right. Take the second signposted path on your right to follow a good track across the moorland all the way to Dolwyddelan Castle, which appears on your right over the brow of the hill. The path to the castle and down to Bryn Tirion, where you pay admission and collect the key, is marked. Retracing your steps is preferable to walking along the A470.

Refreshments

You'll have to bring your own picnic to this walk, although there is a shop in the nearby village of Dolwyddelan (closed on Thursday afternoons).

Public Transport

The Conwy Valley Line is a precious little jewel. Trains run from Llandudno and Blaenau Ffestiniog to Roman Bridge Station WHICH IS A REQUEST STOP (signal the driver or ask the guard).

The Waterfall

Rhaeadr Cynfal

Outline
Ffestiniog - Rhaeadr Cynfal - Ffestiniog

Summary
Steep but attractive paths lead from Ffestiniog through a patch of old sessile oak woodland to a precipitous gorge carved by the Afon Cynfal. The waterfall here (Rhaeadr Cynfal) is not very high, but its top section falls in an almost perfect arch. Nearby is the symmetrical columnar rock known as Huw Llwyd's Pulpit. The return path is through more woodland.

Attractions
This is one of the beauty spots of Wales included in the Celtic Grand Tour of the late 18th and early 19th centuries. The Afon Cynfal falls about one thousand feet in three miles and the Rhaeadr Cynfal is its most spectacular waterfall. The shining force of the water seems to be enhanced by the dark woodland around it. The viewpoint is made safe with steps and handrails. Huw Llwyd's Pulpit is a very special rock hidden deep in the ravine yet standing some 20 feet high in the middle of the river. It is named after Huw Llwyd, who probably lived between 1568 and 1630. He was a soldier and bard from Cynfal Fawr, just south of here. It is on record that he fought in France and Holland with a Welsh regiment raised to fight the Spaniards in the Low Countries. He was also famous as a huntsman, as a chess player, for his knowledge of medicine and for his poetry (his poem "Fox's Counsel" is in the 1977 "Oxford Book of Welsh Verse" — having been translated into English). It is as a conjuror or sorcerer that Huw Llwyd has gone down in legend, however. He reputedly came to this rock (some say at midnight) to meditate, seek inspiration and to raise spirits. Those who followed him said that he called the devil to appear and conversed with him, but Huw Llwyd claimed he was secure from the evil one on his pulpit rock as the devil was afraid of the surrounding water. This tale was incorporated into Thomas Love Peacock's novel "Headlong Hall". Another legend is of Huw Llwyd's wife persuading her brother to follow him and to frighten him by dressing in a white sheet and making fearsome noises. Huw Llwyd didn't flinch, turning on the spirit and telling it that if it was a good spirit it wouldn't wish to harm him, while if it were a bad spirit it wouldn't be able to anyway. Perhaps this is a walk to be taken at night by the light of a full moon.

Route 6

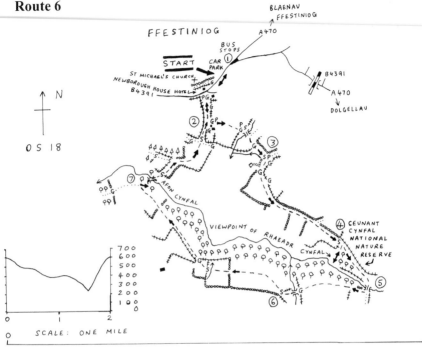

FFESTINIOG

BLAENAU
FFESTINIOG

A470

BUS STOPS

START

CAR PARK

ST MICHAEL'S CHURCH
NEWBOROUGH HOUSE HOTEL
B4391

B4391

A470

DOLGELLAU

VIEWPOINT OF RHAEADR CYNFAL

AFON CYNFAL

CEUNANT CYNFAL NATIONAL NATURE RESERVE

N

O S 18

700
600
500
400
300
200
100
0

0   1   2

SCALE: ONE MILE

Route 6
Rhaeadr Cynfal
2 miles

Start

Ffestiniog, or Llan Ffestiniog, is on the A470 two miles south of Blaenau Ffestiniog, the nearest railway station. (G.R. SH700419)

Route

1. *Walk from the centre of Ffestiniog, where the A470 makes a sharp bend and where there are bus stops and a space for parking cars. Put St. Michael's church on your right and go down the B4391, passing Newborough House Hotel on your right. Turn left through a gate to go down a signposted footpath. Descend as far as the second gate on your left.*

2. *Turn left through the gate to take another signposted footpath. This cuts across a field to a stile beside a gate. Cross this and a subsequent footbridge over a stream. Veer slightly right to go through a gate, then follow the path with a wall on your left.*

3. *Continue over a stile and bear right along a good track to a gate. Go through it to descend gradually to a waymarked stile.*

4. *Cross the stile to enter Ceunant Cynfal National Nature Reserve. Divert down the woodland path on your right to the viewpoint for the waterfalls (Rhaeadr Cynfal). Look for Pulped Huw Llwyd (Huw Lloyd's Pulpit). This pillar of rock, about 20 feet high, stands in the middle of the river, hidden deep in the ravine. Make your way back to the original path and go right to descend gradually to the footbridge over the Afon Cynfal.*

5. *Cross the bridge and turn right along the path which keeps above the trees then veers left to a gate. Go through this gate and over the subsequent footbridge. Walk with a fence on your right to a stile in the corner ahead.*

6. *Turn right over the stile and bear left along the path which goes across a field, through a gap in a wall and over a stream to a stile in the fence ahead. Cross this and bear right down to a gate which leads to a path descending with a fence on your left. When the fence turns left to run uphill, continue descending gradually to go through a gap in a wall. Be careful now to go about 150 yards along this track before taking a narrow zigzag path down to a footbridge across the Afon Cynfal on your right.*

7. *Cross the bridge and climb steeply to a stile. Continue with a fence on your left until a second stile at its top. Bear right here into a field, where you turn left uphill to cross a track and take a stile ahead. This leads to the fenced path which you descended at the start of this walk. Go up it to retrace your steps to Ffestiniog.*

c

31

Refreshments
There are shops in Ffestiniog, otherwise go up the road to Blaenau Ffestiniog.

Public Transport
Ffestiniog is well served by buses, with the No. 1 from Caernarfon, the No. 35 from Dolgellau and the No. 38 from Barmouth all going on to Blaenau Ffestiniog, where there is a railway station (for trains to Llandudno, and Ffestiniog Railway trains to Porthmadog).

Harlech

Harlech

Outline
Harlech Castle - Harlech Beach - Harlech Castle.

Summary
This is a surprisingly strenuous walk, so allow plenty of time for both it and the attractions. Harlech was once the county town of Meirionnydd and its castle has a spectacular situation. Views of the mountains are matched by those of the beautiful coastline. You could spend all day on the beach.

Attractions
The castle and the superb views encourage you to look up and into the distance. If you look far and high enough you might just conjure up a scene from the Mabinogion, to be exact from the story of Branwen, the "white-bosomed" daughter of Llyr, which forms the second Branch of the Mabinogi, that great literary work of Celtic genius now available in English translations especially for children. Harlech Castle is set on Twr Branwen, or Branwen's Tower. Bendigeidfran (Bran the Blessed) was her brother and king over the whole isle of Britain. One afternoon, as he was seated upon the rock at Harlech overlooking the sea, he saw 13 ships coming from the south of Ireland. They brought Matholwch, King of Ireland, seeking the hand of Branwen in a marriage that would unite and strengthen the two islands. Matholwch was taken to the royal court at Aberffraw (Anglesey), where he met Branwen ('fairest maiden in the world") and slept with her. When Efnisien, her half-brother, discovered what had happened, he maimed Matholwch's horses, causing the Irish king to prepare to return home (with Branwen) insulted. Bran offered fresh horses plus gold and silver and peace seemed to be restored. Matholwch still showed signs of resentment at the subsequent feast, however, so Bran offered him further reparation in the form of a magical cauldron that could restore life to a slain warrior, but leaving him dumb. This Cauldron of Rebirth came from Ireland originally and Matholwch was glad to retrieve it. Branwen went back to Ireland with her husband and soon bore him a son, called Gwern.

In the second year of their marriage Matholwch was forced to avenge what his subjects still saw as his disgrace in Wales by driving Branwen from his bedroom and setting her to work in the kitchen under a cruel butcher. Contact with Wales was suppressed and this situation lasted three years until Branwen contrived that word should reach her brother by teaching a starling to carry a message to Bran. Leaving seven men as stewards in Britain, Bran left for Ireland with a mighty host. As the deep water wasn't wide in those days and no ship could contain him, Bran waded across. The Irish saw the forest of sails and retreated inland behind a river. Bran made himself into a bridge over this river for his army to cross it and force Matholwch to sue for peace. The Irish treacherously tried to hide armed men in flour bags at the peace conference but Efnisien spotted the ruse and squeezed each "sack of flour" to death. The kingship of Ireland was settled upon Gwern, but Efnisien threw the boy in the fire, causing a fight. With the Cauldron of Rebirth on their side the Irish were gaining numerical advantage until Efnisien

continued on p36

33

Route 7

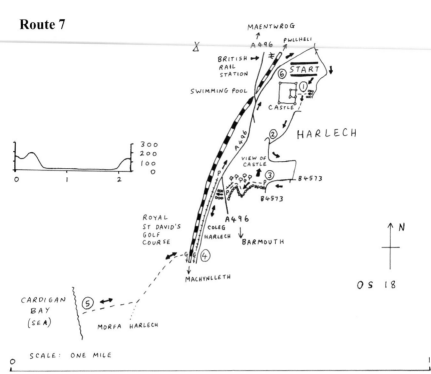

MAENTWROG
A496
PWLLHELI
BRITISH RAIL STATION
START
⑥
SWIMMING POOL
CASTLE
①
②
HARLECH
A496
VIEW OF CASTLE
P
③
B4573
B4573
ROYAL ST DAVID'S GOLF COURSE
A496
COLEG HARLECH
BARMOUTH
MACHYNLLETH
④
CARDIGAN BAY (SEA)
⑤
MORFA HARLECH

300
200
100
0
0 · 1 · 2

↑ N

OS 18

SCALE: ONE MILE
0 ─────────────── 1

Looking north from Harlech

34

Route 7

Harlech

Start

Start from the playground in front of the entrance to Harlech Castle. A car park is nearby, while buses stop just around the corner and below on the road to the British Rail station. Harlech is on the Cambrian Coast Line between Machynlleth and Pwllheli and on the A496 between Barmouth and Maentwrog. The castle dominates the main road and railway, but actually lies below much of the town, on whose side is its entrance. (G.R. SH582312)

Route

1. Face the castle and go left across the car park. Go down to the statue just past the castle on your right. This is the statue of "The Two Kings" by Ivor Roberts-Jones. Go ahead down the road which descends steeply to a junction.

2. Turn left up an old lane which passes below the B4573 and bends right to reach Harlech's High Street. Turn right along this to pass a nursery garden on your right and reach a signposted footpath.

3. Turn right along the signposted footpath, but stay here awhile to admire the classic view of Harlech Castle on your right. Continue down the path beside a wall on your left to finish with steps leading to the A496. Cross this road carefully and take the path opposite to reach a quiet access lane. Turn left along this lane, with the railway on your right and Coleg Harlech (and Theatr Ardudwy) on your left. Look out for a white gate on your right.

4. Turn right through the gate and cross the railway carefully. Go through a second gate and look out for golf balls on the Royal St. David's Golf Course. Follow the path which soon bears left to a fork. Go right to climb over the dunes and reach the beach.

5. When you've had enough of the beach, retrace your steps across the railway and along the lane past Coleg Harlech. This time, go ahead to the junction with the A496 and maintain your direction along its pavement, with the railway on your left and the castle on your right. Do not go over the level crossing, but do fork right below the castle.

6. Continue past the Castle Watergate on your right and the railway station on your left. Turn right up a lane which winds steeply back towards the castle. Take a path on your right to return to the children's playground.

Refreshments

You'll find plenty of places to choose from in Harlech.

Public Transport

The No. 38 bus which runs between Barmouth and Blaenau Ffestiniog will drop you in the centre of Harlech near the start of this walk. The Cambrian Coast Railway Line is always recommended even if it means that you join this route at 6.

continued from p33

pretended to be one of the Irish dead, was cast into the cauldron and took the opportunity to destroy both it and himself by stretching against its walls until it burst.

Seven men returned to Britain. Bran was too badly wounded to go, so he ordered his head to be cut off and carried back, eventually to be buried under the White Tower in London, facing France. First, however, Bran's head was to spend seven years being feasted at Harlech and listening to the songs of the birds of Rhiannon. The statue of "The Two Kings" near the start of this walk shows Bran bearing the body of his nephew Gwern, symbolising the sorrowful burden that love can be and lamenting the folly and carnage of war.

The story of Harlech Castle is just as dramatic. It was built by Edward I to consolidate his conquest of Wales in 1283. Designed for efficient defence by a small garrison, it was tested by Owain Glyndwr's patriotic war in 1403. Slow starvation was the only tactic that could take it, with Glyndwr's men preventing supplies from boats reaching the gate at the bottom of the cliff which was then approachable by water. Surrender followed in 1404 and Glyndwr celebrated by holding a parliament here in 1405. As the tide of war flowed against him, it was Glyndwr's family's turn to be besieged. Facing starvation, they surrendered in 1408 and Henry IV took Glyndwr's wife, Margaret, and two of their daughters prisoner.

Harlech's finest hour came in the Wars of the Roses when, in 1468, it became the last Lancastrian stronghold to surrender to the Yorkists. It was this noble resistance that inspired the song "Men of Harlech". The Civil War between Charles I and Parliament resulted in a similar distinction, with the victorious Parliamentarians only causing token damage to the castle, much against their usual habits. Take the opportunity to visit the castle and climb the 143 steps to the top of the left inner turret of the gatehouse. The view will repay your exertions. It will also impress upon you the exceptional growth of the sand dunes here since the 13th century. They are still growing. You'll have to descend to find the 15 different kinds of orchid that survive in them. Finally, find out what's on at Theatr Ardudwy, adjacent to Coleg Harlech, a residential centre for adult education. You may wish to stay at Harlech, which also has an indoor heated swimming pool and a campsite.

Maes Artro

Outline
Maes Artro - Railway Halt - Shell Island -Llanbedr - Maes Artro.

Summary
An easy walk, mostly along a quiet access road. This is made exciting, however, by its proximity to Llanbedr's Royal Aerospace Establishment and the potential for a race against the tide when it uses a causeway across a tidal estuary to reach Shell Island.

Attractions
Maes Artro used to be an R.A.F. camp, with barracks, offices and mess-halls. It is now a craft village catering for the many tourists who visit the Cambrian Coast. Apart from the craft workshops, which offer pottery, leatherwork, weaving, knitting and jewellery, there is a "village of yesteryear" with re-created traditional Welsh shops and an aquarium stocked with local marine life, with many species of fish, crabs, lobster and octopus. You can also experience an air raid and hear the sirens and bombs dropping in an original World War II air raid shelter, visit an R.A.F. museum, see the reproduction Spitfire from the television series "Piece of Cake" and visit the childrens' playgrounds. These range from a sand pit to an assault course.

The plod to Mochras (Shell Island) is well worth it, although it is really a peninsula, not an island. It was cut off at its northern end when the Earl of Winchelsea had a channel dug through the marshy ground here in 1819. This diverted the Afon Artro, which previously flowed south. The river's old course is now silted up. The island is a delightful place for bathing from sandy beaches and for camping near wild strawberries. It is the 200 kinds of shells that have been identified here that have given it its name. Look out too for migratory birds, including terns, oyster catchers, shelducks (which love to nest in old rabbit holes), sandpipers, black-headed gulls, gold crested plovers, dunlin and herons. Please do not pick the many wild flowers, including the orchids. If you're lucky you may see a seal — or a giant turtle. It was just north of here, towards Harlech, that a giant leatherback turtle was washed ashore in 1988. Weighing 2016 lbs and measuring almost nine feet in length it is the world's largest sea turtle, a fact recognised by the "Guinness Book of Records". The turtle, a male, died when it became entangled in whelk fishing lines. It is now the centre of a major exhibition at the National Museum of Wales, Cardiff.

If you have time to visit the village of Llanbedr, take a look inside the old church. This houses a rare Bronze Age stone with spiral ornamentation.

Route 8

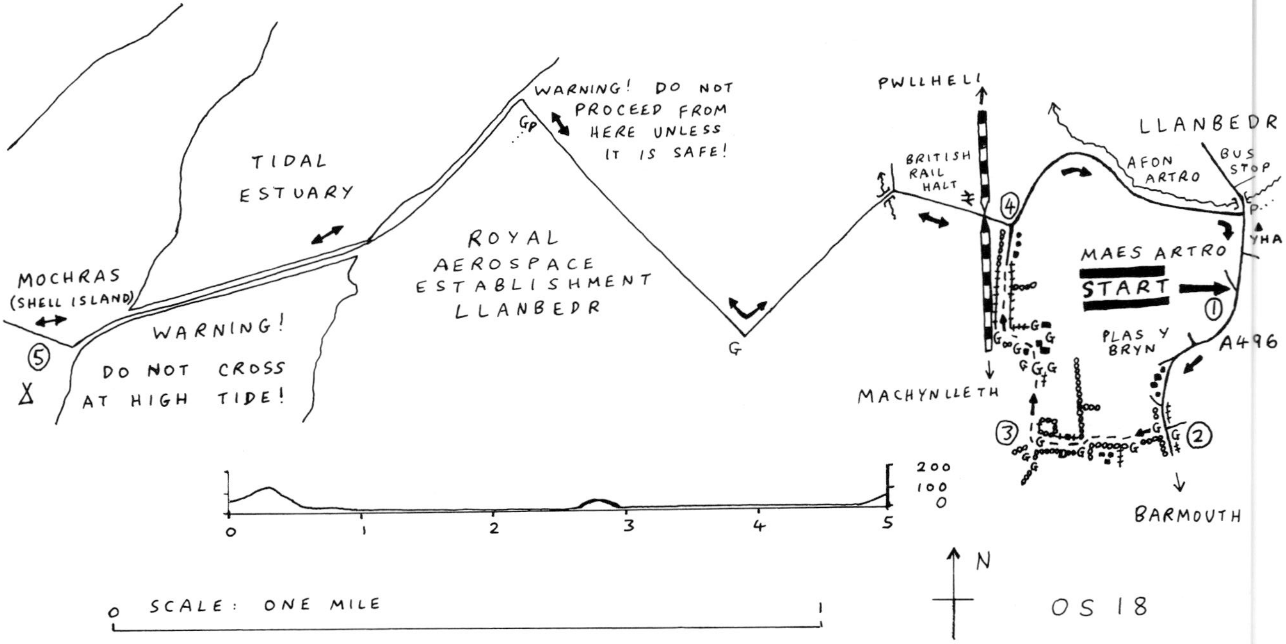

LLANBEDR

AFON ARTRO

BUS STOP

YHA

MAES ARTRO

START

① A496

PLAS Y BRYN

② BARMOUTH

③

④

PWLLHELI

BRITISH RAIL HALT

MACHYNLLETH

WARNING! DO NOT PROCEED FROM HERE UNLESS IT IS SAFE!

Gp

G

ROYAL AEROSPACE ESTABLISHMENT LLANBEDR

TIDAL ESTUARY

WARNING! DO NOT CROSS AT HIGH TIDE!

MOCHRAS (SHELL ISLAND)

⑤

N

OS 18

200
100

0 — 1 — 2 — 3 — 4 — 5

0 SCALE: ONE MILE

38

Route 8

Maes Artro

5 miles

Start

Maes Artro is a craft village famous for its childrens' play area at the side of the A496 just south of Llanbedr. This village, which is served by both a bus and railway, is near the coast between Barmouth and Harlech. Cars can be parked at Maes Artro (admission fee). (G.R. SH585266)

Route

1. From the entrance to Maes Artro, go right along the A496, taking care of the traffic. Pass the access lane to Plas y Bryn on your right, then two access turnings to a group of buildings and the Llanbedr road sign. Go ahead with a wall on your right until the first gate in it.

2. Turn right through the gate in the wall to follow a path running down the left hand side of a field. Maintain your direction to follow this path out of the corner ahead to pass a house on your right and a ruin on your left. Go ahead through a gate across the path.

3. Turn right to follow the track to a farm. Go through the farmyard and bear left. Turn right along the track to walk parallel with the railway on your left to a road.

4. Turn left along the road, taking care at the level crossing. Pass the British Rail halt on your right and go left at a fork to take the bridge over a stream. Follow the road to a bend where the entrance gate to the Royal Aerospace Establishment, Llanbedr, is facing you. Potential spies among you will now know to conceal any cameras as the Official Secrets Act prohibits unauthorised photography of this place. Turn right to take the road to its end, which may be into deep water, so be warned! Look for a sign marking the end of the "county road". This is near a gate giving access to a signposted footpath on your left. The important sign is ahead of you, where the road bears left across the tidal estuary to Shell Island. There should be a board here stating the safe times to cross. Do not proceed unless it is safe! There are other ways to Shell Island (such as the signposted path passed on your left — later on it bears a warning to "look right, low flying aircraft") but none are reliably safe and the road will get you there more quickly.

5. Having explored Shell Island, retrace your steps to Llanbedr's British Rail halt. Continue along the lane to reach the village of Llanbedr, just across the bridge over the Afon Artro on your left. Go right along the A496 to pass the youth hostel on your left and return to Maes Artro on your right.

Refreshments

Maes Arto can provide all you need, as can the facilities on Shell Island. There are also shops in the village of Llanbedr.

Public Transport

Llanbedr has a halt on the Cambrian Coast Railway Line (from Machynlleth to Pwllheli). This halt is passed along this route. There is also a bus (No. 38) to the village from Barmouth and Blaenau Ffestiniog.

Spitfire at Llanbedr (Route 8)

40

Bala Lake

Outline
Snowdonia National Park Visitor Centre - Bala Lake Railway Station - Lakeside Path - Picnic Place - Tomen y Bala - Snowdonia National Park Visitor Centre.

Summary
A gentle walk which gives a flavour of the largest natural lake in Wales and allows for a ride on the Bala Lake Railway, one of the "Great Little Trains of Wales". Bala is a historic town that has retained its Welshness.

Attractions
Lakes are an essential part of an attractive landscape and they don't come any bigger in Wales than Llyn Tegid, Bala Lake. It is four and a half miles long and two-thirds of a mile wide. A modern centre for watersports, the lake is also one of those lakes with a monster. Like Loch Ness, it is in a long rift valley, extending to Tywyn. Originally called Anghenfil but now dubbed "Teggy", the monster has been seen several times, with the last recorded sighting in the summer of 1983. Its large body is said to be at least eight feet long, with dark, shiny skin. The lake does have the distinction of being the only home in Great Britain of the gwyniaid or Alpine fish, a member of the salmon family and trapped here since the end of the Ice Age.

    Wales is the land of legend and Llyn Tegid is the subject of the legend of a wicked king who lived in a palace where the lake is now. He was so wicked that a voice like a bird's warned him that vengeance would come in the third generation. At last the day came of a party to celebrate the birth of the wicked king's first grandson. A harpist was brought to provide entertainment. During an interval the harpist was led by a bird's voice up to the top of a hill. "Vengeance will come" repeated the bird. The harpist awoke to find the valley, including the palace, flooded and his harp floating towards him on the water. Another legend explains that the lake was named after Tegid, who was drowned here by his enemies.

    The Bala Lake Railway extends four and a half miles from Llanuwchllyn, just south of the lake, to the Bala Station visited by this walk. This was merely a lakeside halt before the British Rail line closed in 1965, however. The town station was to the north (Station Road) on the branch line to Blaenau Ffestiniog. Where this branch met the mainline was Bala Junction Station. There is something special about the present Bala Station. Ask one of the engine drivers and they'll confirm sighting a strange family for ever bent down examining the grass here for four leaf clovers. Once we found 108 four leaf clovers at this spot.

    Walking back up Bala's broad, tree-lined High Street, notice the statue of Thomas Edward Ellis (1859-99). As Member of Parliament for Meirionnydd, he was the Chief Liberal Whip. Just around the corner is Tomen y Bala, the motte of a medieval castle which affords splendid views of the town.

Route 9

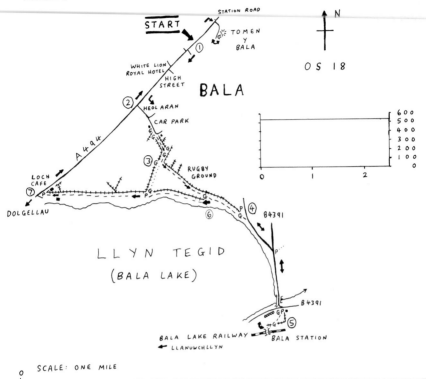

START

STATION ROAD

TOMEN Y BALA

N

OS 18

WHITE LION ROYAL HOTEL

HIGH STREET

BALA

HEOL ARAN

CAR PARK

A 494

RUGBY GROUND

LOCH CAFE

DOLGELLAU

B4391

LLYN TEGID

(BALA LAKE)

B4391

BALA LAKE RAILWAY

LLANUWCHLLYN

G.P.

BALA STATION

SCALE: ONE MILE

600
500
400
300
200
100
0

0   1   2

0   1

42

Route 9
Bala Lake

Start

Bala is easy to reach by bus (No. 94) from Dolgellau or Wrexham. Motorists will find the town on the A494 on the northern side of Bala Lake. Bala used to be easy to reach by train too, on the line from Ruabon to the old Barmouth Junction, plus a branch line to Blaenau Ffestiniog. You can relive a little of this period in the summer by taking the Bala Lake Railway from Llanuwchllyn to join this walk at its half way point. Its start is the Snowdonia National Park Visitor Centre in Bala High Street, opposite the bus stop and a statue. (G.R. SH927361)

Route

1. *With your back to the Snowdonia National Park Visitor Centre, go left along Bala High Street, passing the White Lion Royal Hotel on your right.*

2. *Turn left up Heol Aran, pass the car park on your left and veer right along the footpath to Bala Lake, passing Ystad Cae Bach on your left. Bear right with this path through a gate.*

3. *Ignoring a path ahead, turn left to pass a rugby ground behind the fence on your left. Continue through a gate towards a road.*

4. *Bear right along the road. Keep right when it joins the B4391 and go ahead across a bridge over the River Dee (Afon Dyfrdwy). When the new road bears left take the old, disused, road ahead to a lane. Cross the lane to a gate and follow the signposted footpath to Bala Station (Bala Lake Railway).*

5. *Retrace your steps (or start the walk, if arriving by train) from the station to the B4391 and the bridge over the Dee. Continue by forking left to the gate at the start of the footpath around the edge of Bala Lake (Llyn Tegid) on your left. Follow this path until it forks.*

6. *Fork left to walk with the lake on your left and a fence on your right. Pass a gate, through which runs a signposted footpath, on your right and continue past the Lake Warden's office and the public conveniences on your left. Ahead of you is a picnic place with boats for hire. Your path reaches the A494 at a signpost near the Loch Cafe.*

7. *Turn right to follow the pavement of the A494 into Bala. Continue up the High Street past the Snowdonia National Park Visitor Centre to the start of Station Road. Turn right to see the Tomen y Bala and retrace your steps to the start of the walk.*

Refreshments

Plenty of choice in Bala (plus the Loch Cafe).

Public Transport

Bus No. 94 (between Barmouth and Wrexham) stops near the start of this walk. There is a fairly frequent weekday service. This bus will also take you to Llanuwchllyn for the other end of the Bala Lake Railway, should you wish to enjoy this seasonal service (tel. 01678 540666 for further details).

On the Mawddach Estuary

44

Morfa Mawddach

Outline
Morfa Mawddach Station - Mawddach Crescent - Line of Dismantled Railway - Morfa Mawddach Station.

Summary
This is a fairly gentle stroll taking in the Mawddach Estuary and the line of the dismantled railway which ran from Morfa Mawddach (then Barmouth Junction) station to Ruabon (near Wrexham).

Attractions
The Mawddach Estuary is arguably the finest in Europe. The views across it are a joy to behold. Even better views are obtainable from Barmouth Bridge, so do consider extending your walk to follow the footway of this bridge (and pay a small toll if you continue to Barmouth). This bridge was built in 1867 and was saved from marine woodworm in the early 1980s. The Cambrian Coast railway line still uses the bridge but the halt at the start of this walk is now called Morfa Mawddach. It used to be called Barmouth Junction and catered for trains from Manchester via Dolgellau. This trackbed has now been converted into a pleasant walk which is rich in wildlife. The dry conditions of the stone chippings attract birds-foot trefoil, rest harrow, white mullein and ragwort, while hemp agrimony and purple loosestrife are found in the damp at the edge of the path. Red admiral and other butterflies abound, as do birds in the deciduous woodland. Several birds nest in the reedbeds which can grow up to 12 feet in height.

Whilst in the vicinity, don't miss a ride on the Fairbourne Railway.

White Mullein   White   June-Sept

45

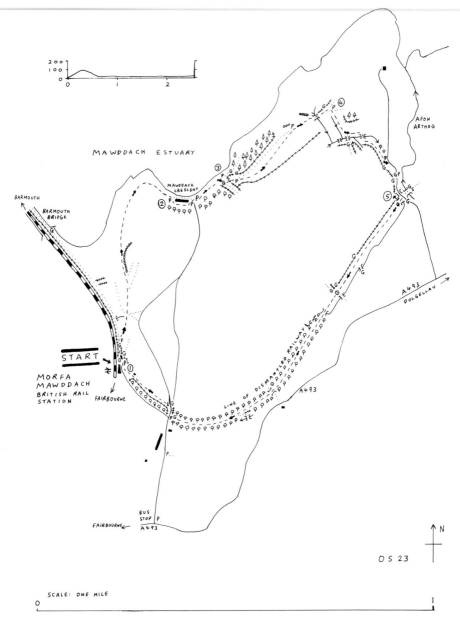

MAWDDACH ESTUARY

MAWDDACH CRESCENT

BARMOUTH

BARMOUTH BRIDGE

AFON ARTHOG

A493 DOLGELLAU

LINE OF DISMANTLED RAILWAY

A493

MORFA MAWDDACH BRITISH RAIL STATION

START

FAIRBOURNE

BUS STOP

FAIRBOURNE A493

N

OS 23

SCALE: ONE MILE

Route 10
Morfa Mawddach
2½ miles

Start

Morfa Mawddach station is on the Cambrian Coast Railway Line on the southern side of Barmouth Bridge. You could walk over the toll bridge from Barmouth or walk up the access lane to the station from the A493 at the No. 28 bus stop between Fairbourne and Arthog. Cars may also be parked at the station, where there are public conveniences. (G.R. SH628143)

Route

1. *Walk north along the path towards the bridge across the estuary to Barmouth, beside the railway on your left. Reach a signpost which marks where your path forks right across a field, around a hillside and right to some houses (Mawddach Crescent). The estuary is on your left.*

2. *Continue past the backs of the houses and along a signposted path as far as a notice saying "Private Bryn Celyn".*

3. *Turn right through a gate and turn left immediately through another gate. Follow the signposted footpath to a second signpost and across a bridge to a third signpost.*

4. *Turn right to walk with a drainage ditch on your right to its confluence with a stream. Do not cross the footbridge ahead. Go left to reach a second footbridge and turn right across it. Go ahead to a lane and bear right along it to the line of the dismantled railway.*

5. *Go right along the trackbed of the old railway all the way back to Morfa Mawddach.*

Refreshments

Go to Fairbourne (or cross the bridge to Barmouth).

Public Transport

Rail will take you to the start of this walk.

Birdsfoot Trefoil   Yellow/Orange

May-Sept

Standing stone

Arthog Standing Stones

Outline

St. Catherine's Church, Arthog - Arthog Waterfalls - Stone Circle - National Trust Car Park - Llynnau Gregennen - Standing Stones - Ffordd Ddu - Arthog Waterfalls - St. Catherine's Church, Arthog.

Summary

The beautiful Llynnau Gregennen (Cregennan Lakes), which are overlooked by Tyrrau Mawr, would be enough to make this walk special. The link between the lakes and the main road (where there is a bus service) is an exceptionally attractive woodland path beside the Arthog Waterfalls which is well worth the effort of a steep climb. Prehistoric men knew this area and, no doubt, venerated it. The evidence is still standing in the form of enigmatic standing stones and a stone circle. If you must travel by car, you could use the National Trust car park and start at No. 3.

Attractions

The Arthog Waterfalls are on the Afon Arthog, which flows from Llyn Cyri to the Mawddach Estuary. The best vantage-point for a view of them is from the bridge halfway up. Keep climbing to see the twin Cregennan Lakes with Tyrrau Mawr (Big Towers) reaching 2,167 feet in the background. These lakes have a deep blue colour and are at around 800 feet above sea level. The private Plas Cregennen is an old hunting lodge made of cedar brought from Canada, dismantled and re-erected just north of the car park.

The Arthog Standing Stones are a ruined ring which has an egg-shape with all the characteristics proposed by Professor Thom, plus two extra stones at the east end and a white quartz boulder which gave me a mild electric shock. The basis of the ring is a half-size 3, 4, 5, right angle triangle. The arcs have radii of 2, 4.5 and 3 megalithic yards and the perimeter has a value of 8.14 megalithic rods. Some stones have, no doubt, been taken to build nearby walls, but three impressive standing stones have survived along this route. They are near the ancient track known as the Ffordd Ddu (Black Road) which leads to Llanegryn.

49

Route 11

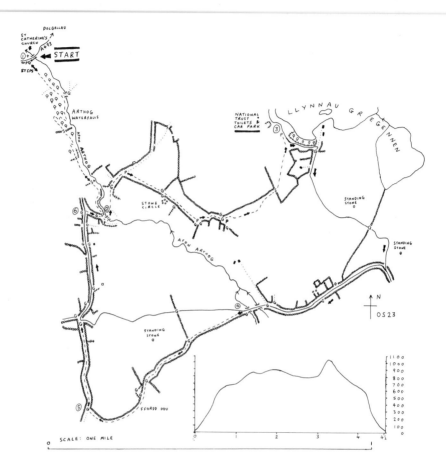

Route 11

Arthog Standing Stones   4½ miles

Start

St. Catherine's Church is on the north side of the A493 just west of the bridge over the river in Arthog. (G.R. SH646146) Motorists may prefer to start from the National Trust car park. (G.R. SH657144)

Route

1. *Cross the road from the church and take the signposted path to the waterfalls. Continue with the river on your left to a stile which gives access to a farm track ahead. Go left along this track a few yards and turn left over a stone footbridge across the Afon Arthog.*

2. *Go ahead to a gate and continue along a walled track to a corner of a field where a signpost points right. Go right beside a wall on your right. Continue through a gate, keep beside the wall on your right and look over it to see the stone circle. Reach a signpost in the next corner and go left between walls to a gate. Go through this and turn left along a signposted path to a slate stile in the corner of two walls. Go over this and bear left to a road, where there is a signpost.*

3. *Turn right along the road with the lake on your left. Follow this road as it bends right through a gate, bears left past a standing stone through a second gate and continues to a junction. Turn sharply right along this road until you cross two bridges over two streams.*

4. *Go ahead up the rough track (the Ffordd Ddu) with a wall on your left. When there is only a wall on your right, keep beside it to a gate in the corner.*

5. *Turn right and go down the track to the road. Continue downhill to a track on the right.*

6. *Turn right along the farm track to reach the stile you crossed on your outward journey. Turn left over it to retrace your steps to the start.*

Refreshments

Bring your own!

Public Transport

Bws Gwynedd service No. 28 runs through Arthog between Tywyn and Dolgellau. Ask the driver to drop you at the church by the bridge.

Near Dolgellau

Dolgellau

Outline
Dolgellau - River Arran - Park Cottage - Nant y Ceunant - Dolgellau.

Summary
Dolgellau is an attractive, concentric town with a children's playground and a putting-green near the bridge over the river Wnion to the north of Y Stryd Fawr (Eldon Square). There is a Snowdonia National Park Information Centre and a Town Trail. This route takes you up the valley of the Arran to the scene of a famous murder at Park Cottage. Here, in the old oak forest, is a glimpse of what most of Snowdonia used to be like. The views from the return path are superb, taking in, from left to right, Rhinogydd, Y Garn, Diffwys and the Arans in the east. You will have a stream to cross. This shouldn't be a problem normally, but wellington boots should be worn in wet weather.

Attractions
Dolgellau has a long history. Owain Glyndwr held a parliament here in 1404, while the Quakers were strong in this area until driven away to Pennsylvania by persecution in the seventeenth century. There was a thriving woollen industry here then, with fulling mills on the river Arran. This walk is especially interesting for its murder, however. It was committed by the last person to be hung in Dolgellau, Cadwaladr Jones. The victim was Sarah Hughes, unmarried, but with two children. Sarah had been missing since June 4th, 1877, but the authorities hadn't bothered to search for her then because they reckoned she had gone to a coal-mining area to earn money. A search was hurriedly arranged when a little girl on an errand for her mother saw an arm floating down the river Afon Arran between Felin Uchaf and Pont yr Arran (the bridge crossed by the Arran Road) on the morning of July 16th. The rest of the body was soon found beneath the bridge near the centre of Dolgellau.

The body had been buried for six weeks, then hurriedly dug up, and thrown into the river when the water-level had risen suddenly after a continuous downpour of rain. Suspicion soon pointed at Cadwaladr Jones, a young married man who lived at Park Cottage, near the river Arran. He had been working away from home during the week at Coed Mwsogog, where the 36 year old Sarah was also employed. Jones soon confessed to the murder when the police came to search his cottage. He led them to the disturbed soil where the body had been buried in the garden.

His wife seems to have guessed that Cadwaladr was guilty and didn't visit him until the night before his execution. A possible motive for the murder was revealed when Sara Hughes' sister, Margaret, said that her deceased sister had been pregnant. The trial took place in Chester, but the execution took place in Dolgellau on November 23rd, 1877. Despite having pleaded that he had struck Sarah in a fit of rage, not meaning to kill her. Jones later confessed that he had planned to murder her. Public opinion remained sympathetic to him, however.

Route 12

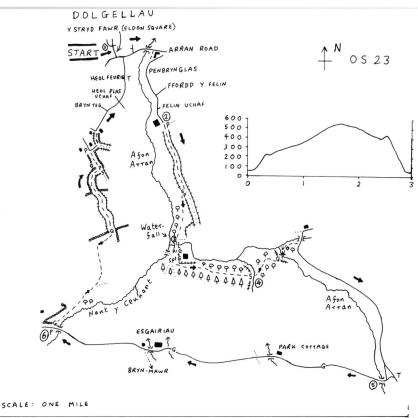

DOLGELLAU
Y STRYD FAWR (ELDON SQUARE)
START ① ARRAN ROAD
HEOL FEURIG T
HEOL PLAS UCHAF
BRYN TEG
PENBRYNGLAS
FFORDD Y FELIN
FELIN UCHAF ② P
Afon Arran
Water-fall
PIG
SPIG
Nant y Ceunant
ESGAIRIAU
BRYN-MAWR
⑥ P T
④
Afon Arran
PARK COTTAGE
⑤ T

N
OS 23

SCALE: ONE MILE

54

Route 12
Dolgellau
3 miles

Start
Y Stryd Fawr (Eldon Square) is in the centre of Dolgellau. This is the capital of Meirionnydd and lies at the junction of the A470 with the A493 and the A494. (G. R. SH728178)

Route

1. *With the Midland Bank on your left (east), go ahead to the end of the square and turn left along Upper Smithfield Street. This leads to the bridge over the Afon Arran and Arran Road. Cross the bridge and turn right to reach an estate road. Go up this, with the river on your right.*

2. *When you reach the top of the road, with the tannery on your right, take the right hand fork. Climb up this steep track until a stile is reached on your right. Cross this to follow the signposted path down to a footbridge ahead, noticing a waterfall on your right.*

3. *Cross this footbridge, but ignore a bridge on your right. Go left along a path at the foot of the forest and climb with it through the trees to a stile. The path crosses a stream here. Normally this isn't a problem, but this is where you will need your wellington boots in wet weather.*

4. *Veer left, then bear right to a gate which gives access to a footbridge. Cross this bridge and take the path which veers left between a building and a ruin, then bears right to a lane. Turn right along this lane. It forks just before a telephone box. Go right to cross a bridge, followed by a cattle grid.*

5. *Follow this lane to Park Cottage, on your right. Continue past another cottage (Esgairiau) and notice the track to Bryn-mawr on your left. Go ahead to a stone bridge, which you cross.*

6. *Take the signposted path on your right and admire the views as you go down to a gate in a wall on your left. Follow the narrow path towards Dolgellau. Ignore a signposted stile on your right, but turn right down a track at the next signpost. Bear left downhill into the town, passing a Roman Catholic church and the Post Office on your right in Heol Feurig. This leads back to the start in Y Stryd Fawr (Eldon Square).*

Refreshments
Although Basil and Dorothy Sayle, who now live in Park Cottage, have offered to serve "murderburgers" along with suitable souvenirs, you'll probably have to eat and drink in Dolgellau, where there is a choice of cafes and shops.

Public Transport
Dolgellau is at the centre of the bus network in Meirionnydd. Long distance routes include the D94 (Wrexham-Barmouth) and the Trawscambria 701 (Cardiff-Bangor).

At the time of writing, the buses stop in Y Stryd Fawr (Eldon Square), but this may be changed when the square is pedestrianised. The car parks are signposted.

Making friends

Dinas Mawddwy

Outline

Meirion Mill - Foel Dinas - Dinas Mawddwy - Meirion Mill

Summary

Forest tracks provide a view over the Dyfi Valley on the first half of this walk, then you descend to visit the village of Dinas Mawddwy. Allow plenty of time for this short walk as it takes in two sets of swings, at Y Plas and at the Meirion Mill.

Attractions

Dinas Mawddwy is an attractive village in an unspoilt corner of the National Park which is steeped in history. King Arthur may have fought his last battle at Camlan just south of the Meirion Mill, where this walk starts. This woollen mill is located in the grounds of the old station and yard of the Mawddwy Railway. Admission is free and there is a mill shop. The playground is excellent (no dogs allowed) and the Old Station Coffee Shop is nearby. Opposite this is an old pack-horse bridge across the Afon Dyfi. The Roman road from Wroxeter to Brithdir probably Crossed the river here too.

The helicopter, Meirion Mill

57

Route 13

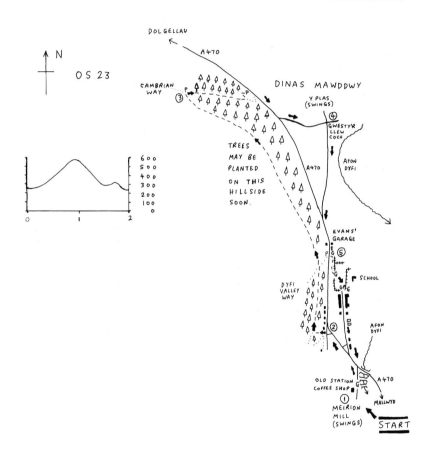

SCALE: ONE MILE

OS 23

DOLGELLAU

A470

CAMBRIAN WAY

③

DINAS MAWDDWY

Y PLAS (SWINGS)

④

GWESTY'R LLEW COCH

AFON DYFI

A470

TREES MAY BE PLANTED ON THIS HILLSIDE SOON.

600
500
400
300
200
100
0

0   1   2

EVANS' GARAGE

⑤

SCHOOL

DYFI VALLEY WAY

②

AFON DYFI

OLD STATION COFFEE SHOP

A470

①

MEIRION MILL (SWINGS)

MALLWYD

START

Route 13
Dinas Mawddwy   2 miles

Start

Meirion Mill is on the A470 one mile north of its junction with the A458 at Mallwyd, about eleven miles east of Dolgellau. (G. R. SH859139)

Route

1. *Walk back from the car park at the Meirion Mill towards the Old Station Coffee Shop, opposite which are steps leading down to the riverbank for a view of the old pack-horse bridge. Climb back up the steps to turn right and go through the old station gates. Bear left up the access road to the A470, away from the river. Turn left along the grassy verge of the A470 until you reach a war memorial in front of a garage on your left.*

2. *Turn left and take the track into the forest, passing the garage on your right. You soon reach a T junction. Go right here to climb gradually to a crosstracks above a second garage. The path which comes downhill from your left and continues across your path to the garage is part of the Dyfi Valley Way, a long distance route of 108 miles from Aberdyfi to Borth via Aran Fawddwy. Maintain your direction along the forest track, which continues to climb gradually. The A470 is below on your right.*

3. *Stop when you reach a public footpath signpost on your right. This marks where another long distance route crosses your path. This is part of the Cambrian Way, here 187 miles from its start in Cardiff and with 87 miles still to go to its northern terminus at Conwy. Turn right to descend with the Cambrian Way to a layby on the A470. Go right along the roadside verge and take the turning on your left into the village of Dinas Mawddwy. Reach a crossroads with the "Gwesty'r Llew Coch" facing you.*

4. *If you want to visit the swings in the Plas, go left. Continue the walk by turning right to pass the inn on your left, then the shop and Post Office on your right. Go ahead to Evans' Garage (Gwyndaf Evans is the rally driver). Go ahead along the pavement of the A470.*

5. *Turn left down a flight of steps and follow the narrow path down to the school. Continue past the school along a road which leads back to the A470 at the Buckley Pines Hotel. Go left along the pavement a few yards, then cross the road carefully back to the Meirion Mill.*

Refreshments

Plenty of choice! The Old Station Coffee Shop can provide drinks, snacks and meals, while drinks are also available in the Meirion Mill. Dinas Mawddwy has a shop, as have the two garages along this route, while the 'Gwesty'r Llew Coch' (Red Lion Inn) is near the Plas swings.

59

Public Transport

Buses are infrequent but they will drop you off right at the Meirion Mill. Current times must be checked, but at the time of writing there are buses from Machynlleth (S18) every Wednesday and Saturday and from Dolgellau (27) every Tuesday and Friday and on Thursdays in the summer. These services allow several hours between buses.

Near Llanegryn

60

Llanegryn

Outline
Llanegryn - Church - Gwastad Meirionydd - Cae'r Mynach - Llanegryn.

Summary
An attractive old church stands on the edge of wild, windswept moorland where fairies have been seen. There is some steady climbing involved, but the paths are good and the return to Llanegryn is made along a quiet farm access lane.

Attractions
There are swings near the start of this walk, so determination will be called for, plus the promise that the swings will still be there at the end. An attractive path above a stream leads to Llanegryn's church. This used to be dedicated to its founder, the seventh century St. Egryn, who may have studied under St. Illtud at Llantwit. The Cistercians of Cymmer Abbey, near Dolgellau, built the present church and a hospital in the 13th century, dedicating it to St. Mary the Virgin. They may also have contributed the elaborate rood loft and screen which were installed here in the 16th century, perhaps being rescued from Cymmer Abbey.

Old records state that fairies have been seen at Gwastad Meirionydd, on the bleak moorland which is crossed by ancient tracks. Perhaps these "fairies" were like the "earthlights" seen near Egryn Abbey, also associated with St. Egryn but north of Barmouth, in 1904/5.

Rood-loft, Llanegryn

Route 14

Route 14
Llanegryn   4¾ miles

Start
Llanegryn is just off the A493 two miles north of Bryncrug. (G.R. SH600054)

Route

1. *Start from the bus stop in Llanegryn. Cars may be parked nearby. Walk east, into the village and turn left when the road bends slightly right BEFORE a telephone box. This turning leads to a gate on your left. Go through it to follow a path over a footbridge to the swings. Go left with the stream on your left to a gate beside a public footpath signpost.*

2. *Cross a lane to go over a stile and continue above the stream on your right. Notice the church across the valley and turn right over a footbridge to reach it. Climb a stile in the wall to visit the church, then leave by the gate on to the road.*

3. *Turn left along the road and turn left again immediately to follow the right of way through a farmyard and beside a wall on your right before descending to cross another footbridge. Keep the stream on your right as you go right through a gate and over three stiles to Blaidd.*

4. *Emerge on an old green lane, or drove road. Turn left uphill and continue to the ruins and crosstracks at Gwastad Meirionydd.*

5. *Bear right along the track which stays beside the wall until it veers away to follow a line of telephone poles across the moorland.*

6. *When the track meets the corner of a fence on your left, turn right along the track which leads to Cae'r Mynach and a lane back to Llanegryn.*

Refreshments
Bring your own!

Public Transport
The No. 28 bus links Llanegryn with Tywyn and Dolgellau.

The grave of Mary Jones

Bryncrug

Outline
Bryncrug - Afon Dysynni - Pen-y-wern -Bryncrug.

Summary
Snowdonia is famous for its mountains, but this is an easy, flat walk, almost at sea level. The views up the Dysynni valley towards Cadair Idris are majestic, however, while you may spot a heron from the embankment path.

Attractions
The chief attraction is the grave of Mary Jones. This is easy to find in the graveyard of Capel Bethlehem, Bryncrug. Mary Jones was born and bred in a remote cottage at Llanfihangel-y-pennant, at the foot of Cadair Idris, but she was to marry Thomas Lewis, a weaver from Bryncrug, settle here and attend the Calvinistic Methodist chapel. Her story has gone around the world as an example of religious devotion. It dates from 1800, when Mary was 16. Mary's ambition was to own a Bible, so that she could study it and commit to memory portions of scripture. She had saved up her pennies for six years and now had enough to buy her Bible. Bibles, especially Welsh Bibles, were very hard to buy, however. Mary was told to make the 30 mile journey to Bala, where the Rev. Thomas Charles had just obtained fresh supplies from London. So she rose before dawn on a spring morning to commence her long walk. Her only pair of shoes were too precious to be ruined by such a trip, so Mary carried them for wearing in Bala and walked in her bare feet. Arriving in Bala that evening, Mary was told that it was too late to see the Rev. Charles that night, so she accepted lodgings at the home of a local preacher. He woke her up before dawn next day and took her to the Rev. Thomas Charles, who was at his desk already. He had disappointing news for Mary. All the Welsh Bibles had been sold and the suppliers had declined to print any more. Mary's story so touched the Rev. Thomas Charles that he gave her his own, personal, copy. This incident also moved him to find the means of supplying the pressing demand for more Bibles both in his own country and in others. Two years later he told the story of Mary Jones to the Committee of the Religious Tract Society. As a result, the British and Foreign Bible Society was established in 1804 and its first resolution was to publish an edition of the Welsh Bible for the use of Welsh Sunday Schools (the first consignment of these Bibles reaching Bala in 1806). The Rev. Thomas Charles never forgot the little bare-footed girl who had walked thirty miles over the mountains to see him. He was to visit her at her home and keep her informed about events elsewhere. Mary died at Bryncrug in 1864, aged 80.

Route 15

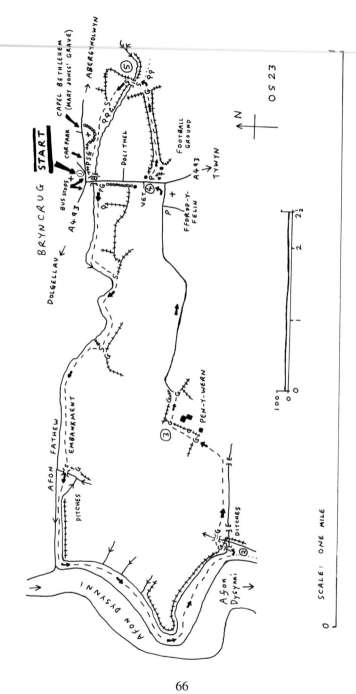

SCALE: ONE MILE

OS 23

Route 15

Bryncrug
2½ miles

Start

Bryncrug is at the junction of the A493 and the B4405 two miles north-east of Tywyn. It is relatively well-served by buses, which stop near the start of this route. (G.R. SH609033)

Route

1. *With your back to St. Matthew's church and facing the bus shelter, go right towards the village shop and turn left to cross the pedestrians' bridge over the Afon Fathew. Look for a kissing-gate and a public footpath signpost across the road on your right. Cross the road carefully and take the signposted path which goes downstream beside the river on your right. When the Afon Fathew meets the Afon Dysynni, turn left to follow the path along the top of the embankment.*

2. *Reach a waymark post at the junction of the embankment path with a path which crosses the flat pasture to Pen-y-wern. Turn left, away from the river, to cross a bridge over a drainage ditch and go ahead through a gate. Turn right to cross a bridge over another drainage ditch, go through a gate and walk ahead. Ignore a plank bridge across the ditch on your right, but notice a second such bridge and turn left away from it, towards a gate. Go through it to pass the farm buildings of Pen-y-wern on your right.*

3. *Take a gate on your right and cross the farmyard to a gate giving access to a lane. Follow this lane back to the A493 at Bryncrug. Go left for a few yards.*

4. *Look for a signposted path across the road on your right. Turn right to cross the road carefully and take this path, which leads to a gate. Bear left to a stile leading to a footbridge. Cross another stile on the far side of the bridge and bear left to a stile in a fence. Go ahead over this and continue below the wall of the graveyard of Capel Bethlehem on your right to reach a stile beside a gate and a signpost. Cross this stile to return to the start of the walk. The entrance to Capel Bethlehem's graveyard (for Mary Jones' grave) is on your right.*

Refreshments

There is a shop in Bryncrug.

Public Transport

Bryncrug has two bus stops for two different bus services. Service No. 28 (which runs between Tywyn and Dolgellau) stops near the Peniarth Arms, on the A493. Service No. 30 (which runs between Tywyn and Minffordd) stops at the bus shelter opposite St. Matthew's church, at the start of this walk. Tywyn has a Railway station and is the terminus of the Talyllyn Railway, whose Rhydyronen Halt serves Bryncrug.

67

Talyllyn Railway

Rhydyronen

Outline
Rhydyronen Station - Braich-y-rhiw - Stream - Rhydyronen Station.

Summary
A short walk up a wild, desolate valley. This will give you the flavour of Snowdonia without moving far from one of the national park's chief tourist attractions, the Talyllyn Railway. Use this "great little train" to reach the start and take a walk which should fit in well with the train timetable.

Attractions
A caravanning and camping site is hardly a tourist attraction but it is a necessity for many families holidaying on a budget. There is a recommended site just across the road from the start of this walk. Just imagine, using the Talyllyn Railway as your local commuter line!

The Talyllyn Railway is, of course, the only proper way of reaching the start of this walk. Its success over the past forty years is a vindication of the magnificent pioneers who refused to let this railway die in 1950. Many other railways have been preserved since, but this was the first.

Slate was the reason why the railway was built in the 1860s. The quarries were near Abergynolwyn and the slate was carried by packhorses to the harbour at Aberdyfi. When a railway connected Aberdyfi with Tywyn, a group of businessmen from Manchester decided to invest in laying a 2 foot 3 inch gauge line from the quarries to connect with it. The first train ran in December 1866, with passenger services commencing the next year.

Its last private owner was Sir Henry Haydn Jones, who promised to keep the line open during his lifetime, which he did when the last quarry closed in 1948. Sir Haydn's death in 1950 would have led to the railway's closure but for the formation of the Talyllyn Railway Preservation Society. The line went under a transformation fuelled by the enthusiasm of voluntary labour. The track has been relaid, bridges strengthened and the station at Abergynolwyn faithfully rebuilt. New locomotives and rolling stock have been purchased and record numbers of passengers carried. Trains run from Easter to October and over Christmas (tel. 01654 710472).

The Talyllyn is more than a railway. Start at its Tywyn Wharf terminus and you can visit a Narrow Gauge Railway Museum. Wharf Station used to be the interchange with the nearby main line for the slate. The passenger terminus used to be Tywyn Pendre, where the engine and carriage sheds are. Rhydyronen Station used to be an intermediate stopping place containing a siding for the loading of slate wagons. The line has terminated at Nant Gwernol since 1976, giving it a total length of $7\frac{1}{4}$ miles.

Route 16

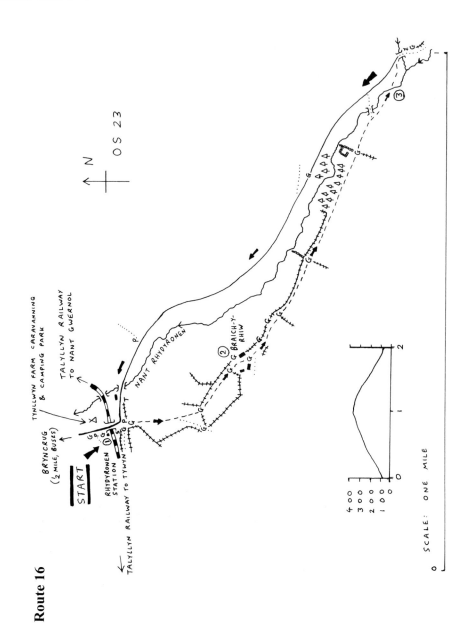

SCALE: ONE MILE

Route 16
Rhydyronen   2 miles

Start
Rhydyronen is a station on the Talyllyn Railway two miles east of Tywyn. It is also served by an access road off the A493 in Bryncrug, less than one mile to the north, where there is a car park and bus services. (G.R. SH615022)

Route
1. *From Rhydyronen Station, go right along the road over the bridge across the Talyllyn Railway. When the road bends left, go straight ahead up a signposted path, going through a field gate. Fork left to a gate in the top corner of this field and continue to the farmyard at Braich-y-rhiw.*

2. *Go ahead up the valley with the stream below the fence on your left. Pass a plantation of trees on your left and go ahead through a gate to open moorland. Keep the stream on your left and notice a footbridge across it. DO NOT USE THIS FOOTBRIDGE AS IT IS PRIVATE!*

3. *The right-of-way crosses the stream about 150 yards above the footbridge. Climb up to a lane and turn left. Go down this lane, with the stream now on your left, all the way back to Rhydyronen Station.*

Refreshments
None here, but at Tywyn Wharf and Abergynolwyn stations.

Public Transport
Take the Talyllyn Railway's narrow gauge train straight to the start of this walk. If you come out of season, take a bus to Bryncrug (No. 28 from Dolgellau or Tywyn, No. 30 from Minffordd or Tywyn).

Near Rhydyronen

71

Afon Cynfal   (Route 6)

Useful information

Approximate mileage of each walk from Dolgellau via main roads.

Route	Dolgellau
1	**50**
2	**38**
3	**30**
4	**24**
5	**26**
6	**17**
7	**18**
8	**15**
9	**17**
10	**8**
11	**6**
12	**0**
13	**10**
14	**16**
15	**17**
16	**18**

Routes in order of difficulty

None of these walks would be strenuous to an experienced walker. The following grading is made in the context of a Family Walks book and is done with the fairly active six or seven year old in mind.

Easy Walks

Route 3 *Betws-y-Coed (1¾ miles)*
Route 4 *Beddgelert (1¾ miles)*
Route 8 *Maes Artro (5 miles)*
Route 9 *Bala Lake (2½ miles)*
Route 10 *Morfa Mawddach (2½ miles)*
Route 15 *Bryncrug (2½ miles)*

Moderately difficult

Route 5 *Dolwyddelan Castle (3⅓ miles)*
Route 7 *Harlech (2¼ miles)*
Route 12 *Dolgellau (3 miles)*
Route 13 *Dinas Mawddwy (2 miles)*
Route 16 *Rhydyronen (2 miles)*

More Strenuous

Route 1 *Conwy Mountain (4¼ miles)*
Route 2 *Llanberis (2⅔ miles)*
Route 6 *Rhaeadr Cynfal (2 miles)*
Route 11 *Arthog Standing Stones (4½ miles)*
Route 14 *Llanegryn (4¾ miles)*

Public Transport

This is more than an item of information. This is an appeal. Please leave your car (if you have one) at home and enjoy touring Snowdonia by public transport. The environmental benefits of doing so are great and Gwynedd County Council is to be applauded for its determination to maintain its public transport network. Even if you camp, you'll find campsites (such as at Harlech) close enough to a railway station or a bus stop for you to manage all the luggage (I know, I've done it!). British Rail will bring you here via Chester (for the North Wales Coast Line, which serves Conwy, and the Conwy Valley Line, which serves Betws-y-Coed — another place with a campsite near its station) or Shrewsbury and Machynlleth (for the Cambrian Coast Line, which serves Harlech). There are also buses, including the Traws Cambria (701) from Cardiff and the No. 94 from Wrexham to Dolgellau. Once in Snowdonia, there is the Bws Gwynedd network, including the "Snowdon Sherpa" services, the British Rail lines along the Cambrian Coast between Machynlleth and Pwllheli, the North Wales Coast between Llandudno Junction and Bangor and the Conwy Valley, between Llandudno Junction and Blaenau Ffestiniog. Most of all, there are the "Great Little Trains", such as the Talyllyn Railway, the Bala Lake Railway, the Ffestiniog Railway and the Llanberis Lake Railway. The Snowdon Mountain Railway will take you to the summit of Snowdon. Make the most of your holiday by buying a Rover ticket. There are several types on offer. The North and Mid Wales Rover covers both buses and trains for a week and can include travel from Chester or Shrewsbury. Details of this and bargain bus tickets are available from Arriva Cymru, Imperial Buildings, Llandudno Junction, Gwynedd, tel. 01492 592111. Don't forget about Family Rail Cards. Many attractions allow reduced admission fees for train or bus ticket holders. If you're just making a day trip by bus within Gwynedd, buy a bargain Gwynedd Bus Rover (a family ticket is available). A complete set of bus timetable leaflets and a public transport map is available for just a 9" x 6" S.A.E. from the County Planning Officer, Gwynedd County Council, County Offices, Caernarfon, Gwynedd, LL55 1SH, tel. 01286 679535.

Tourist Information Addresses

Snowdonia National Park Authority, National Park Office, Penrhyndeudraeth, Gwynedd, LL48 6LS. Tel. (01766) 770274.
Tourist Information Centre, North Wales Regional Office, 77 Conway Road, Colwyn Bay, Clwyd, LL29 7LN. Tel. (01492) 533419.
Tourist Information Centre, Mid Wales Regional Office, Canolfan Owain Glyndwr, Machynlleth, Powys, SY20 8EE. Tel. (01654) 702401.
There are Tourist Information Centres at Aberdyfi, Bala, Beddgelert, Betws-y-Coed, Conwy, Dinas Mawddwy, Dolgellau, Harlech and Llanberis.

Wet weather alternatives. Completely or partly under cover.

It does rain in Snowdonia, so it is useful to know where to go if it's too wet for a walk. The following list is not comprehensive and current tourist information should be consulted. It is arranged by its proximity to each walk.
Walk 1: *Conwy Castle; Conwy Visitor Centre; Aberconwy House; Aquarium; Smallest House; Plas Mawr; Harbour Lightship; Boat Trips.*

Walk 2: *Snowdon Mountain Railway; Llanberis Lake Railway; Oriel Eyri; Welsh Slate Museum.*

Walk 3: *Conwy Valley Railway Museum; Gwydir Castle; Trefriw Woollen Mill; Penmachno Woollen Mill.*

Walk 4: *Sygun Copper Mine; Maritime Museum (Porthmadog); Welsh Highland Railway (Porthmadog).*

Walk 5: *Dolwyddelan Castle; Conwy Valley Line; Llechwedd Slate Caverns; Gloddfa Ganol Slate Mine.*

Walk 6: *Ffestiniog Railway; Llechwedd Slate Caverns; Gloddfa Ganol Slate Mine; Ffestiniog Pumped Storage Scheme.*

Walks 7 & 8: *Harlech Castle; Maes Artro; Cambrian Coast Line; Harlech Swimming Pool; Theatr Ardudwy; Old Llanfair Slate Caverns; Portmeirion Italianate Village.*

Walk 9: *Bala Lake Railway.*

Walks 10 & 11: *Cambrian Coast Line; Fairbourne Railway and Butterfly Safari.*

Walk 12: *Penmaenpool Nature Information Centre; Coed-y-Brenin Visitor Centre; Centre for Alternative Technology.*

Walk 13: *Meirion Mill.*

Walks 14, 15 & 16: *Talyllyn Railway and Museum; Holgates Honey Farm, Tywyn; Tywyn Swimming Pool; Tywyn Cinema.*

Welsh Words and their meanings

Aber — river-mouth, confluence
Afon — river
Bach, fach — small
Bryn — hill
Bwlch — pass, defile
Cae — field
Caer — fort
Carreg — rock
Cefn — ridge
Coch — red
Coed — woodland
Cwm — mountain valley

Dinas — fort, city
Dol, ddol — meadow
Fawr, mawr — big
Ffynnon — well, spring
Foel, moel — rounded hill
Llan — church, sacred enclosure
Llyn — lake
Nant — brook, stream
Pen — top, head
Plas — mansion
Pont, bont — bridge
Ucha, uchaf — upper

Fairbourne Railway (Route 10)

View across Mawddach Estuary (Route 11)

THE FAMILY WALKS SERIES

The publishers welcome suggestions for further titles in this series; and will be pleased to consider manuscripts relating to Derbyshire from new or established authors.

Scarthin Books of Cromford, in the Peak District, are also leading new, second-hand and antiquarian booksellers, and are eager to purchase specialised material, both ancient and modern.
Contact Dr. D. J. Mitchell, 01629 823272
Visit our website: www.scarthinbooks.demon.co.uk